Sonnetizer

Sonnetizer

Poems by

Cameron Morse

© 2023 Cameron Morse. All rights reserved.
This material may not be reproduced in any form, published,
reprinted, recorded, performed, broadcast,
rewritten, or redistributed without
the explicit permission of Cameron Morse.
All such actions are strictly prohibited by law.

Cover design by Shay Culligan

ISBN: 978-1-63980-244-9

Kelsay Books
502 South 1040 East, A-119
American Fork, Utah 84003
Kelsaybooks.com

for my children

Acknowledgments

Thanks to the editors of the magazines in which the following poems first appeared (some in earlier forms) or are slated to appear soon:

BigCityLit: "The Crawlspace"
Blue Moon Literary & Art Review: "Me and My Children," "Parent Teacher," "Jixian"
The Broadkill Review: "The Geese"
Clementine Unbound: "New Galleries"
The Coop: "Birdsong"
DASH Literary Journal: "Stirrings," "Falling Between"
Eunoia Review: "How Long," "My Lazy Bones"
The Handy, Uncapped Pen: "*The Life Aquatic*"
The Indianapolis Review: "Induction," "Quiet at Breakfast"
The MockingOwl Roost: "The Flung Man"
the museum of americana: "Fall Class"
New Feathers Anthology: "Bone Marrow"
North of Oxford: "Amber Alert"
Orange Blossom Review: "Black Cat"
Otoliths: "The Other World Is Our World," "The Next Flight," "Symptom or Side Effect"
Pirene's Fountain: "Temodar at Midnight," "Grief Is Talking," "Secrets Whispered to the Wind"
Post Grad Journal: "The Crux"
Quail Bell: "In Passing," "Foreign Tongue"
RockPaperPoem: "The Fuss"
Tipton Poetry Journal: "Lili"
Two Hawks Quarterly: "Dark Comedy," "Blood Panel," "The Birthday Balloon"
Uppagus: "Enough's Enough"
Verse-Virtual: "No Way"
Visions International: "At Home with Dad," "Because We Are Born"

Wilderness House Literary Review: "Staring at the Screen," "Lost in the Showroom"
Willawaw Journal: "Winter Storm Brain Scan," "Nocturne"

Contents

How Long	13
No Way	14
Dark Comedy	15
The Crawlspace	16
Me and My Children	17
My Lazy Bones	18
Staring at the Screen	19
The Crux	20
At Home with Dad	21
Amber Alert	22
In Passing	23
Parent Teacher	24
Black Cat	25
The Life Aquatic	26
Because We Are Born	27
Induction	28
Stirrings	29
Falling Between	30
The Face in the Tree	31
The Other World Is Our World	32
Winter Storm Brain Scan	33
Nocturne	34
Temodar at Midnight	35
The Fuss	36
Fall Class	37
Bone Marrow	38
The Geese	39
Spring Rain	40
Birdsong	41
Hellraiser	42
Time Is a Bridge	43
The Next Flight	44

Foreign Tongue	45
The Etymology of Anguish	46
Lili	47
Jixian	48
The Cough	49
Symptom or Side Effect	50
There Are Foxes	51
The Deadbeat Meets His Better Half	52
Butterfly Needle	53
Hollow Ice	54
Grief Is Talking	55
Quiet at Breakfast	56
Waiting Around at Santa Fe Trail Park	57
Blood Panel	58
Infant Insomniac	59
Lost in the Showroom	60
The Birthday Balloon	61
To Theo, Age 4	62
Secrets Whispered to the Wind	63
New Galleries	64
The Nestling	65
Apple Blossom	66
Enough's Enough	67
The Flung Man	68

How Long

How long does it take for the brush
to be cleared, before one can utter a word,
how much longer before the cut down
can stand again on shaky legs? The conscience
can only absorb so much, the child
answer for only so many sins before the rain
breaks its fist against the wall. How long
before I realize there is no rush, I may meander
through the smashed field of side effects,
a meadow at sunset where the deer stare back at us
extraterrestrials on our own home planet?
I want the rain to fall on me forever, overwhelm
my meagerly squawking mouth, my tiny
child's voice raised, scarcely clearing the din.

No Way

There's no way to rush recovery.
The body waits to feel all right,
for the stars in its spine to align.
Meanwhile, lie still. Listen
to the furnace. Its sigh goes on
for minutes. Afterwards,
the room feels warm. It's December
out there in the dark, but not
inside the house. Not beneath the blanket.
There's no way to rush inspiration:
The spirit either stirs inside or it doesn't.
Outside, the wind is zero miles
per hour. December waits.
There's no way to rush recovery.

Dark Comedy

Temodar, did I dream the doctor said
it would be you, not the tumor,
it would be you who murders me?
Dear friend, what times we have had:
Lots of good fun that is funny. I am today
two years older than Bill Hicks was
when his pancreas ate him alive, as I still am,
pretty much, as heavy as my foot is
to lift in the Temodar dark of February
before dawn, as long as the razor strop rasp
of its drag: Pendulous slab of beef I have
had to raise, purposely lift into silence
as I ambulate. My lymphocytes lie dead
in the dark pancreas my doctor says will eat me.

The Crawlspace

Thunder creaks in the crawlspace.
The house speaks to me nights I have
trouble sleeping, its tongue pierced by nails.
Lightning haunts my window, lightning
without rain. If only I could sleep
and be healed, sleep without dreams.
Breathe without dread. But I am on my hands
and my knees always in the dark spaces
beyond the ladder, above and beyond,
in the distance between your hand
and my thigh, the lightning and the horizon.
The house cringes then cries out.
My son is afraid of the thunder. I explain
the lightning is still far, far away.

Me and My Children

Boy with the cereal box on your head,
girl with the cheesy grin, window
in the shape of a fan ablaze, a blazing window,
I am a mote of dust in the kitchen
that is lit at sunrise and otherwise invisible
in my own life. Bacon smoke, the smell
of ground coffee and the screech of the grinding.
My children are the wind that kicks up
the window curtain. Toppling garbage cans
up and down the block. The squirrels that disfigure
a perfect pumpkin. They are board meetings
of stuffed animals, top bunk aerial photographs
of squiggly train tracks while I, always,
am just the eye behind the lens.

My Lazy Bones

The full moon glares at me
in my dark corner. For months,
I ignore her. I pile the covers
against my face and sleep.
I would rather forget my dreams
than try to remember. For months,
I mouth the bullet hole. Snow falls
in the window curtains, slowly
burying the driveway. I keep waiting
for an intermission. For a long time,
I run on empty. Not really ready
to believe the purr of my engine may
hush among the myriad other cars
that have run off the road.

Staring at the Screen

Snowfall a staticky screen at the window,
an interrupted sentence. I have lost
reception, drifting beyond the tower's reach
the way my left hand's lost its connection
to the source: Cut off from the electrical
wellspring of the brain, my rowboat rocks.
My blood oscillates on a colder current of ice.
Frequently, I find it difficult to believe
in anything. The clear signal I started out with
has ruptured. There are stark intervals
of silence, rolling blackouts, and the silk screen
of distances does not part. Inside the house,
inside the cocoon sewn into the hem
of my robe, I hold a grudge, a boiled grub.

The Crux

Sunrise cracks its orange egg
in the crux of branches: It is crucial
that the sun rise. Illuminating
the terraces, back yards of snow
and shadow, dogs let out to do
their business. Sun fries in a crux
of branches. A dark skillet, cast
iron, casts the glow by which I know
the frost from the scrubby yellow
grass of my yard. Yellow fries
of light before breakfast are good,
an orange god hanging in the scaffolding
of night even better, even if the cold
is not healthy for my feet.

At Home with Dad

You only get so many sunsets, I say,
and rain is special that falls while the sun
is setting. It's electric rain, the pins
and needles of an awareness. Thunder
is the voice of lightning, the baritone
in the opera of the sky, the growl
of the bear. It is the sound that lightning makes
when it is so lonely it could die
because every tree it touches bursts
into a torch, an effigy of itself burning.
Lightning is a torch, I say, that you can use
when it's really dark outside. A flashlight
on the nightstand. But come on out
of that tree. That's a bad idea.

Amber Alert

An automated voice says hi every time
I pass the blue house on the corner. Otherwise,
no one out here in the cold wants to be
my friend. In February brightness, branch
shadows drop an estuary in the intersection.
A streetlight bisects 41st Street. Hawks
on the lookout for lunch meat. "Hi," says
the voice, and a tree's murder caws
at the intrusion. In these houses we hoard
darker shadows, illusions. Afterwards,
an Amber Alert hurts my ears during a romp
with the kids, interrupting Truck Tunes
on my iPhone. We have to explain
why some children get lost, go missing.

In Passing

The tracks ring a glass bell when wet,
thin siren, now that snowmelt's bathed again
in the basement. My father visits
after dark whom I haven't seen in a decade.
In cobwebs, the abandoned calico
of yesterday curls up in my lap and pulls loose
the fibers in denim. A bell chimes
and I am no longer a chicken, hypnotized
by the headlights of the oncoming
traffic, cascade of cars rolling over my shoulders.
I am a fox in the chicken coop.
A neighbor lady spots me and alerts each passerby.
I am, in passing, also a neighbor lady,
keeping an eye out for foxes.

Parent Teacher

Night of the meeting I scrunch into my
child-sized chair and get ready
for a talking to. In the empty classroom,
two women have been waiting
for a while. The full moon idles out
in the silent parking lot. I want to wipe
the spider webs out of their eyes,
these ladies of the night. I want to tell them
a good story that will whisk us off
to sleep. Another parent is always backed up
behind, laying on an angry horn.
I would prefer to hover an inch above
the pavement. Slam on the brakes,
daybreak. Caterwauling makes my skin crawl.

Black Cat

Thought is like that: a step
barefoot on the back
deck. No moon but light
entombed in cloud. A shape
drops from the fencepost.
Something in the dark makes
sense to you now. A cat
you cannot be sure is black
flickers across the yard.
It's like looking for your glasses.
All you can do is reach
into a possible place, the nightstand,
or the living room rug,
until the blind hand sees a sprig.

The Life Aquatic

New baby and no function in my left hand
means I may not hold her. No wonder
The Life Aquatic makes me cry in my laundry
basket and I write down, "Infra 5 Orchestra
Version," in a red marker. Paint swatches—
"seaside villa, sunbaked brick, incredible
white"—a deck of cards arrayed before me:
Pick a card, pick any card. I should have
been killed as an undergrad in Grand Rapids,
crossing some black parking lot. How many
times had I walked to Celebration Cinema
to sit alone in an empty theater and weep
during *The Darjeeling Limited?* Samples
of paint bloom on the dark wall of my bedroom.

Because We Are Born

Because we are born blind rodents
without fur and root in the bright, shivering
room for what we have no name for,
not from hunger but because the trial and error
of millennia has channeled through us
countless dead infants, we latch right away
in the clutched arms of a drowsy woman
torn practically in half by our arrival. Because
we arrive riven, the rubbery connection
severed with a pair of sterilized scissors,
there is in our DNA a strong desire to be held
and if no one will hold us, Jesus does,
whose arms are always open, cracked open
wide to the lamb that bleats in our DNA.

Induction

Six months back on chemo and my
limp worsens toward bedtime.
Left hand's shot, so there goes the cane,
there goes the wheelchair.
What's it to be then, in the interim?
Scheduled the meeting with my daughter
for the day after tomorrow
Lili determined for her water not to break
before the induction. Lead me.
I don't know where the hell I'm going.
Induce, conclude, from these particulars.
The kiss of existence is fading
on my forehead, forever disappearing,
handed over to a final daughter.

Stirrings

The leaves are still dead but not
the breeze that moves in them
and I was here, too, once:
One more breath in the leaves.
Defying death briefly in the afternoon
on the last day in February
a breeze stirs. I may be ready to ask again
some of the old questions. I may be
warmed into knowing. Cool air cups
my ear, a handmade funnel,
paper cup. I used to be good at hearing
through a crowded room.
I was good at being born, not just dying
all the time. I could be born, too.

Falling Between

Cancer is a late train, near the end
of the line, somewhere in the desert
of stars for these elders two, three
times my age, these sagging dinosaurs.
I locate myself in the gap, falling
between the sink and the countertop.
I envy the infamous cancer kid, a gold
fish going belly up on the car ride

home from the pet store, but also I want
to be these careful gardeners with bird
baths and binoculars. In the waiting room
of warts and liver spots, the bathroom
door's been barred, deadbolted since I arrived
for my blood draw, my stick in the arm.

The Face in the Tree

The elder eyes are buried in the gnarls
of memory. Knots impossible to pick apart
with the teeth. Like the decision to have
no further children. Put down a pet dog.
Who can unearth themselves from grief,
lift their gaze when necessary to yay,
and again, another day? There are trees
on the brightening ridge. Who can

untangle the understory we wade through
our whole lives, trying to reach the tracks
and find a clear crossing? The eyes,
we're told, are windows. If so, what do we see
in them but our own reflection? Doppelgänger,
ghost brother, long unheard from friend.

The Other World Is Our World

Knowing where we are begins as an inkling
of cars passing up ahead before I can make out
the sign. Our street goes through,
our payment. Our breakthrough begins
before we can make sense of an illegible hand.
From another angle, our world is other-
worldly. Our shadows cast bodies
and not the other way around.

A train stopped in the woods stretches on
and on, heading off our crossing.
Its headlights are light in daylight. We were always
walking home, always to begin with,
snow banks of broken glass, brittle reefs
along the disappearing sidewalk.

Winter Storm Brain Scan

In this dream I wake up to premedicate
for the wake, the black trees
wedding gowned, brides in the fallout
from radiation. Imagine me
prancing insensate though this brain
snow in my birthday suit, my suite
the trundling insides of the machine
shop loud with elbow grease and blood

redacting the sentence of my death.
Hear me out in bloops and bleeps
naked groom getting ready to denude
the dead bird, a black suit sliding
bullet through the chamber, the magnetic
tube of resonant mechanical waves.

Nocturne

Daughter I wake to discover, "bolt
upright" in bed, not the one I laid you in,
quite a night you've had, some fight
with the lions in your den. Bombed out
porcupine hairdo daughter, are you
all right? I don't like the sound of that
chain smoke rasp in your voice,
the husky cowboy ghost possessing you.

I tell my computer to sleep and lie down
beside it. Tiny gears go on whirring.
A little while clicks off. Trombone tock
of the train station clock, comings
and goings, gongs in the valley
of the temple, the dimple in my skull.

Temodar at Midnight

My stomach is a goldfish gurgling in a bowl
of dark flames. Poor pet fish burn victim,
my tummy hurts. My son can call for mommy
when he wets the bed, and she staggers

through the door. Strips it in the dark. I wake
to discover the dank mound on bathroom floor.
Temodar's my mommy. She drags an extra blanket
over my shivering legs and plants a wet kiss

on my forehead. She's the furnace kicking on
with a bang at midnight. She helps me sit
to pee beside the moon-ignited shower curtain.
Temodar leaves the door ajar to my swimming room

in case I call out in the dark water for a hand
to hold me under, help me drown.

The Fuss

The house holds its breath
and waits for the train
to pass, for the hysterical wailing
to subside into silence. Angry

when you first had sex
that that was it, what all the fuss
was about, if you could call that sex.
The house makes a big fuss

about the photos on its mantle, the gray
smear of an ultrasound,
if you could call that an ultrasound.
The train is sentimental. You know trains,

always dragging their feet, longing
to go back and change things.

Fall Class

Glassworks of winter branches
as if the trees might shatter, the way
my elbow split at the touch
of cement. Brittle season, depleted

bone marrow bodes ill for the bone.
A student harbors hurt feelings:
The grudge ripens. Fragile winter flower.
The flow of tractor trailers

below my balcony window is impervious
to viral infection. The voice inside
you doesn't know what to say this morning.
The furnace kicks on in the basement.

Otherwise, the silence is constricted:
Thicker the sock, colder the foot inside it.

Bone Marrow

Treatment eats tomorrow
out of my bones, Temodar at the dark
dinner table chomps. The truck
flakes with my shipment of sleep.

A blizzard erases the footprints
of my children. My eyes
agape are helpless now. Blindfold
of oblivion fall, please, fall.

Say please for the strawberry ice
cream. There is black gunk
in the cracked chicken bone. Gross.
Treatments like trick or treat.

One blind turn at the dead end of night
wake up one day this will all be over.

The Geese

Twilight opens a window
on the drive home from Legend of Asia
with the kids in their car seats
for thousands of disparate geese flocks

for vast swarms to storm the house
momentarily vying for victory
over disbelief. I try explaining why that
letter of the alphabet to Theo,

who is learning his ABC's, but can never
get a word in edgewise. I am overwhelmed
by their letters flapping crosswise
in this window between diagnosis and death.

Sun down, a helicopter crashed
just an inch beyond the burning horizon.

Spring Rain

It's technically spring. The magnolias pouting.
But even my kids know to hurry inside
when the first silver coins land on the deck rail.
To duck in and wash their hands for dinner.

Even if the slot machine of heaven gushed, or
spilled its guts, into my dusty hands,
I doubt I'd know what else to do but stand there
like an idiot in my skin soaking through

my skin, an empty scabbard, empty socket,
skull talker, please, give me another chance. If given
a choice, I'd have had more children, engendered
a new swarm. Disease is underrated.

So is splendor, downpour, the magnolias dropping
their underthings in my oil-stained driveway.

Birdsong

The difference is not that it is light
when I wake but birdsong
added to the darkness
lets me know I am no longer alone.

Lili is usually not in bed beside me
when my iPhone vibrates
on the nightstand. One of our children is,
or no one, and I have to go searching

for my wife, passed out
somewhere with the newborn
clutched to her chest, Gigi,
who wakes often to check on us

and make sure we haven't wandered off
in the dark: lost, among stars.

Hellraiser

Scrawny infant squawking daughter
unswaddled for the car seat
in a more winter than spring rain,
welcome to the world, hellraiser.
March is bipolar in Missouri. Welcome
to this corner of the world. Here is
my thumb. You cannot seem to locate
your own. Let's do something about those

maniacally flapping hands, those
dagger-length fingernails. What a nuisance
it is to be born. Regurgitated on dry land.
Exposed to the elements. Let's adjust
the thermostat. Sandwich the breast.
Get some meat on those bones.

Time Is a Bridge

The bridge delivers me to the other side.
I am a letter, in this life. My contents
are for your eyes only. The bridge carries me
in her mailbag. I am an arrow pointing
toward you, the lost direction I was going,
the railroad crossing. My heart and hope
to die. There have been so many points
of no return, I'm terrified to think

how far I've come, I've strayed away
from home. The truth is time is a bridge
that collapses the moment you cross it,
it bursts into flame. Cinder sizzling in the dark,
icy current carrying every letter I've ever written
downstream into a maelstrom of mistakes.

The Next Flight

I will not know my thought:
I must wait for my thought, my flight.
My sister struggling to keep up holds on
to her hurt years among the pagodas,
abandoned. I am running out of time
to make amends for the people I have been
and hurt, the unthought hours
rolling over, going belly up in the shipyard.

I will not know. How could I ever
escape the manifest I myself am on?
My adult sister settling in to the seat beside me,
asks if I have any memories of her
as a girl. I run for my thought. This time
I am out of takes off without me.

Foreign Tongue

The tongue is in your mouth
when you speak it, learning its contours
by feel, blindly rolling over the wet
roof, the soft palate and gums. So what?
Is it strange then that I married a foreigner?
A strange girl inhabited me. Her words
warped my doorframe. Her tongue
in the temple bell that tolls in the valley

at nightfall. Her language wandered
feline streets among the lit shops
of families that boil pork and bean sprouts
in the aisle then turn in on cots nudged
just out of sight, glimpsed among the bags,
the jars and boxes on the shelf.

The Etymology of Anguish

If the etymology of *anguish* is a tight place,
mine is Dongguan during the second-to-last
chaste summer of my life: I am 20 years old.
Prompt, eleven o'clock rain showers naked
among the mango trees. The t-shirt I run in
is red and tight. I run, and the rain runs a red
streak down the mango lane, but there is no
escape from the compound, the rowhouse.

I play Ping-Pong with Mom in a windowless room.
My red darkens. Sweat stiffens my shirt.
Nobody notices how horny I am but the checkout
girl toward whom I extend my first box
of condoms, the cigarettes I hadn't figured out
how to inhale, in my innocence, anguish.

Lili

In Yantai, Lili rode on the back of my
bicycle, an arm wrapped around my waist,
and I pedaled us to the beach on our
first date, not knowing she'd fallen asleep
as a girl and rolled off the rooftop.
Her mom fed the pet dog to the hospital director.
Her mother, who could always find
a vein, was a master seamstress.

My wife mastered raw meat before I could
boil water. With her cousin, she liked
to torture cockroaches. I knew none
of these things when I asked her
to marry me: the idyllic childhood fields
of rapeseed, half-repressed memories.

Jixian

Where the body finds itself at home
in the bright seam of afternoon, I have
afternooned in brightness, crossing
a dusty intersection of tuk-tuks
toward a prayer tree in the temple yard
in Jixian. Ribbons lifting lightly, yes,
and eaves which wasps cruise, but also
inside that warm palm the chill blade

of a breeze has again suggested a double
edge to my happiness: a cold coin
in the alms bowl of the sun. Whether the idea
is spring, or sprung, or autumn, God knows.
I know only I am at ease in my body:
My body thinks it's OK to stay here a while.

The Cough

I develop my chemo cough like a photograph
in the dark room of my chest. I keep
the cough in my chest of drawers,
out of reach of the children, my rattling bottle,
gravel road. My old neurooncologist
once suggested to Mom it would be the treatment
that kills me, not the tumor. The thunder
of my body gathers in the branches of the lungs.

Something is forming in the dark, or some
one. My children are right to feel afraid. My dog
is right to scamper under the grand piano.
What the end is I cannot conclude from the now
available data. April's outburst of rain, ice,
all hand sleight, mixed signals. Killing kindness.

Symptom or Side Effect

Electrical waves crash over my head,
the beachhead of my brain, prickly stubble
of sand, or I have the kind of sudden
fatigue that makes a Mason jar from the dish rack
heavier than a car battery. How to describe this
to my oncologist? Symptom or side effect?
Twilight makes it orange on the horizon,
orange as an orangutan or the handgun

the boy at the playground yesterday
shot me in the eye with and my wife on the park
bench, nursing beneath a muslin cloth
and my son on the rock wall, my daughter in the child
safety swing. Ha! I laughed: No one was left
to push him. He called and called and no one came.

There Are Foxes

My son disappears up ahead. I lag behind
in my sandals. Wayward men in army jackets
roughen the streets of our neighborhood,
stray dogs. There are foxes. My boy abandons me
to them and his little sister cannot keep up.
The sky is thinking about rain when my son
runs up ahead, sidestepping cars. My attic
turbines pick up speed from the quickening wind.

A dark parade of clouds fills the sky with dread.
A neighbor lady reports she saw a small boy
turn downhill. Toward the bottoms, I am
developing quite the limp because of my son.
If Theo reaches home before the rain, I'm going
to give him the scolding of a lifetime.

The Deadbeat Meets His Better Half

Red meat hand, inflatable foot. Because of my
blood-puddled left half, I have to ask
my right to handle it, and she does,
for the most part. Her helping hand is stronger
for helping: Singlehandedly
lifting our daughter from the top bunk,
pulling the absent father from the hammock
of a sling into a cradle for baby,

a complete circuit: My Dad never meant
to neglect me. His mother was deaf (true story).
She couldn't hear him crying,
so he has never stopped crying. Also,
he has never heard me with his perfect hearing,
no matter what I say.

Butterfly Needle

No offense to your kiddos smirking in red
jerseys and grass-fed kneepads, but I prefer
sitting on the right side of the room
while your needle roots for a sloppy vein
in the crease of my arm. There's a painting
in the hallway I can fix my eyes on.
It's just a little forest water stepping over
some rocks, but I'm thankful for the diversion.

At the beginning of my journey, I stepped
over some rocks. My job was to track
the butterfly needle through a forest of exam
rooms until nightfall when at last it would
alight upon the blossom of my arm and sip
its bloody Mary and murder me repeatedly.

Hollow Ice

In the nightmare I notice the fingers
of my left hand are hollow ice
cubes, the kind the maker messes up on,
an accurate description of me also,
it could be argued, with the wet, ragged
branch of tumor draped across the brain wire
that services my entire west side but most
narrowly the neighborhood called Hand.

Long story short: I tuck my fingers in
to a splint before bed. In the dream,
for some reason, I'm already in the hospital.
The nurse I show acts like it's none of her
business, so I wander down around the offices,
the bustling corridor, looking for a bandage.

Grief Is Talking

I stop dead at breakfast. Break off,
grief is talking through my four-year-old.
He remembers the basement we used to
play in, our LEGOS on the unused
changing table. Our Hot Wheels rode
the ramps of leftover floor planks.
In the basement, Daddy sang and played
the guitar. Not so anymore, the contra-

diction I can observe at breakfast opening
an unshuttable door in Theo's brain
to the beautiful basement of lost things,
melodies. I still have the cracked Alvarez
Dad had ordered for my 16th birthday.
As it splits apart, the songs escape.

Quiet at Breakfast

What direction the wind is, is wet
whether to walk in. Bereft
of vitamin D. I stand accused of just
wanting go out—so what if it's
cold and rainy, I am also to blame
for being quiet at breakfast.
Walking out of one too many movies.
Tom Bull's widow indulges in day-
dreams of apocalypse. America
treats itself to freedom, an extra helping
of loneliness. Eliot's March to April rain
cringes. I cross the bleak parking lot.
Looking for a drop box, a safe distance. If,
and, or but. Beholden to no one.

Waiting Around at Santa Fe Trail Park

Clouds waving tentacles of white flame
above the tunnels and the slides
of the playground Omi and I are left to
wait at. For a long time, we have it
entirely to ourselves, an empty playground,
so I don't have to think about the spectacle
I'm making: scrunching, or scooting
into the port-holed submarine, the cancer
patient cradling a shriveled left arm
on the spiral down through the birth canal.
Omi squeals and bumbles about.
The clouds wave hello to her, goodbye to me,
the white octopus clouds. This effort
I'm making to squeeze through is laughter to her.

Blood Panel

The phlebotomist must like the taste
of my blood, even if I can no longer hold
the cotton ball while she reaches for a roll
of co-bind. She takes so much out of me
to save for later, enough to stock a pantry,
feed an army. It's a wonder I can stand
and pull down my sleeves after she fills her vials.
I must be virile. Spouting in the vacuum
of her tube, even if I avert my eyes, searching
for distraction, before her needle dives.
There are no paintings in her bedroom, only
another chair with wings, her calendar. Photos.
I must remind her of her firstborn
in the woods, her howling second birth.

Infant Insomniac

My palm drums on her swaddled shoulder.
The cadence convinces her, a drip
of rain reverberated in the downspout.
Wade forward into the dark, quiet water
that came before you were born,
regurgitated on dry shore. Allow the layers
of water to pile overhead. Be covered,
caressed, a loose carcass in the dark mouth
of swallowed water. Shallows melting away
behind us, shadows of twilight abandoned
for the deep end of the pool. The darkest
corner of the bag invites you, a white
mouse with red eyes, my little insomniac,
blindsided by the black paw, the heavy suitcase.

Lost in the Showroom

You can imagine in the labyrinth constructed
to confuse the minotaur that you are the minotaur,
lugging the head of a bull through compact
kitchenettes and TV rooms. On your way back
from the bathroom, you are surprised
that all the books are now in Swedish, though
you have never been to Sweden
and outside the rat's maze it's actually Miriam, Kansas.
What the hell, right? Your hooves are stilettos
clicking among the shrieks of the young, echoing
through plasterboard displays of the family
you have lost somewhere in the twists and turns,
the switchback of years trying to find your way back,
and rejoin your mother, sister, daughter, wife.

The Birthday Balloon

The birthday balloon leaps among chandeliers
in the vaulted ceiling of the dining room. Buoyant
with our yearly wishes, yearnings. My clawing
children have to take turns pinning it under a pillow
during reading time, or tacking its restless energy
between bunks. At last, however, it falls to me,
whose balloon it ultimately is, because I am turning
35, to stow our upwardly mobile friend in a dark,
unreachable corner of the monster closet so the kids
can relax, and shut the door behind it, still pressing
its happily foiled helium nose to whatever heights
available, and say goodnight, knowing sad fate of all
balloons is either to sink over the course of a few days
or shrink: a red a dot disappearing over the tree line.

To Theo, Age 4

I want to set you down at the pasture's
edge, my feral child. I would fend off the flock
of combs aimed at your tangled mane,
but your dinosaur excavator pants we have
long since stopped thinking of as pajamas
are still too dirty for you to wear to school today
and your light blue hoodie is smeared. I want
desperately to side with you alone against them
all in this melee called society, called every-
body gets what everybody wants, but you still
cannot pull Isaiah's hair for being noisy
during naptime. You still can't push your sister
for pushing down your cathedral of magnet
tiles, even though I can see the justice in it.

Secrets Whispered to the Wind

Wind-frazzled apple tree, watch your tongue.
These white petals you're dropping are
heavy hints our time here is finished, it might,
in fact, be time to move on. White petals
fill up the wicker lap of my patio chair
as if to say: this seat is taken. I am open
to suggestion but its power is one I, too,
possess, or am possessed by. The spirit fritters away
its measly allowance of white petals. Goes bust,
belly up. The tree blooms, it swells
with blossoms, but something has to give.
Some last bastion. Who can resist? Secrets whispered
to the wind. These petals in the grass are eyelids.
Spring is here, blink and you'll miss it.

New Galleries

The dead limb lost its bark a long time ago,
a middle finger to the interstate in my back yard.
The interstate sighs. It's been here before.
It will be here again. Besides, the limb
is no longer alive. It's just a monument
to what was. Pumped full of bullet holes
by the carpenters. Who open new galleries
in the sky. Inside the limb, the interstate
is not so loud. The carpenters are too hard at work
to notice the sirens, the whale song of the big rigs.
Their mandibles whirring, they do not listen.
The tree lowers its finger and I mistake
their work for woodrot as my chainsaw smiles
through the clouds of sawdust.

The Nestling

Easy or not, these are the ways the world has
of making you stop in your tracks.
The sky screams. Not a murder but a single
solitary crow sails over Main Street.
Omi stomps up ahead in glittery pink Sketchers,
my dandelion princess pumping her meaty
little arms. Developing quite the god complex.
The crow goes about its business. It pays
no mind. The fledgling pinched in its beak
cheeps in cool blue April brightness. Missouri
offers narrow windows of good walking weather
between the indoor seasons of fire and ice.
Omi doesn't hear the scream. Neighbors slow down
and wave through the windows of passing cars.

Apple Blossom

—for a second daughter

Apple blossom puts the loss
before the blood, apple blossom in the labor room
where it belongs. Our tree is a family
of blossoms, a syndrome:
We all say the same thing. I put my hand
in your hand. Look down
to avoid the epidural
needles of rain. I almost fainted
when Naomi was born. What is that
a symptom of? Before you were born,
the tree knew it would have
to bloom. Springtime knew, and now
that you're here we shiver in the brightness
of April blossoms and ache.

Enough's Enough

Clouds bat the sun's ball of crystal yarn
with fluffy white paws. Wind tousles
the chimes. That's its part. Whether the result
is resonant or the grating of forks
and knives is up to the chimes. The sun
shines, that's what it does, and the clouds
push their wheelchairs back and forth
across the sky. The light lowers its legs
into the chair, sits down and stands up again
after a restful ride. It's nice to kick back
in the passenger seat and take it easy
but after a while, when enough is enough,
the hands itch for the steering wheel,
and the wheel wants to be back in the hands.

The Flung Man

I can no longer find the abandoned
house from whose fence corner
terraced above I-70, I watched the flung man
dug out of an embankment
in a kneeling prayer circle of firefighters.
I watched, myself encircled by
a small gathering of nameless neighbors
at sundown but also alone
because my own son would not follow,
afraid to miss dinner. I introduced myself
to strangers. The house, one said,
was abandoned, eight years, so no need
to worry about trespassing; the man down there
I already knew, was me.

About the Author

Cameron Morse is Senior Reviews editor at Harbor Review and the author of nine collections of poetry. His first collection, *Fall Risk,* won Glass Lyre Press's 2018 Best Book Award. His poems have been published in numerous magazines, including *New Letters, Bridge Eight, South Dakota Review, Portland Review,* and *The Indianapolis Review.* He holds an MFA from the University of Kansas City-Missouri and lives in Independence, Missouri, with his wife Lili and three children.

www.ingramcontent.com/pod-product-compliance
Lightning Source LLC
Chambersburg PA
CBHW030914170426
43193CB00009BA/841